ITALIANS

in America

ITALIANS

in America

Ronald P. Grossman
with Martha Savaglio

 Lerner Publications Company • Minneapolis

Page 2: The Romana family sews doll dresses in their home, early 1900s.

Front cover: Millie and Tony Serpe, owners of Serpe's Bakery, with their 6-year-old granddaughter Angelina Bargelski, in their booth at St. Anthony's Italian Festival in Wilmington, Delaware, June 1992

Back cover: Detail of tile fragments decorating sculptor Simon Rodia's Nuestro Pueblo, *Los Angeles, California*

1993 REVISED EDITION

Library of Congress Cataloging-in-Publication Data

Grossman, Ronald P.
    Italians in America / Ronald P. Grossman. — Rev. ed.
        p.   cm. — (In America series)
    Includes index.
    Summary: Discusses the contributions of Italian explorers and immigrants to the history and civilization of the United States.
    ISBN 0-8225-0244-5 (lib. bdg.)
    ISBN 0-8225-1040-5 (pbk.)
    1. Italian Americans—Juvenile literature. [1. Italian Americans.] I. Savaglio, Martha. II. Title. III. Series.
E184.I8G86   1993
973'.0451—dc20   92-31325
                                           CIP
                                            AC

Manufactured in the United States of America

10   11   12   13   14   15   98   97   96   95   94   93

CONTENTS

1
EXPLORATION AND EARLY SETTLEMENT

When we think of the Italian influence in America, we may think of opera, Italian art and architecture, or the Roman Catholic church. Italians have brought many popular foods to the United States, from broccoli and cauliflower to pizza and french fries. Italian-American educators, politicians, and writers have shaped the way people think. According to the 1990 U.S. census, there are 14.7 million Italian Americans. Their influence has been great, despite prejudices held against them. Large-scale Italian immigration to the United States did not begin until 1880. Yet certain Italians are identified with American history from its earliest days.

The Navigators

During the Middle Ages (476–1450), Europeans didn't know about the Western Hemisphere. Their contact with other nations was limited to India, Africa, China, and Japan. Europe's sailors traveled east to find valuable gems, gold, and spices. They sailed all the way around the southern tip of Africa to reach the eastern lands.

Christopher Columbus (1451–1506), an Italian navigator, believed there was a shorter route to the

Christopher Columbus was the first of several Italian sailors to explore the Americas. His voyages established new, lasting contact between Europe and North and South America.

Indies—a western route. In 1492 he set sail on what was to be the famous voyage that established lasting contact between Europe and the North and South American continents.

In all, Columbus made four voyages west, yet he never did reach the Indies. Instead he reached land unknown to him, and he explored the coasts of the islands we now call Cuba, Hispaniola, Jamaica, and Puerto Rico. On his third and fourth voyages, he reached the South and Central American mainlands. These lands were inhabited by native people who had lived there for thousands of years. But to Europeans, the land was a "New World."

Amerigo Vespucci

America owes its name to another Italian navigator, Amerigo Vespucci (1454–1512). Several years after
Columbus's first voyage, Vespucci explored the coast
of what we know as South America. He published
an account of his journey, and because the account
was so popular, Amerigo Vespucci's name came to be
associated with the unfamiliar land. Mapmakers of
the early 1500s used his name—Amerigo—to refer to
the continents. Eventually the two continents became
known as the Americas.

The Italian explorer John Cabot (born Giovanni
Caboto) also sought a western route to the Indies.
His 1497 voyage was no more successful than those of
Columbus, but Cabot sailed farther north and reached
Newfoundland and Cape Breton Island, now part of
Nova Scotia. John Cabot's son, Sebastian Cabot, ex-
plored the North and South American coasts, hoping
to find gold. Not much is known about the Italian
navigator and pirate Giovanni da Verrazano. Histori-
ans believe that in 1523 Verrazano entered the North

American mainland by way of New York Harbor, and that he reached the Hudson River and explored the New England coast.

The Missionaries

Besides the famous sailors, other Italians were among the first Europeans to explore North America. They were Roman Catholic missionaries, people sent by the church to convert American natives to the Christian faith.

Father Marcos de Niza came to America in 1531 to work among the native people of Peru and Mexico. He was fascinated by their stories of cities to the north. In 1539 he traveled north, into the present-day states of Arizona and New Mexico, where he met tribes of native people called the Zuni and the Pima. Father Marcos's reports of this journey interested the Spanish general Francisco Coronado. On Coronado's famous exploration of the American Southwest, Father Marcos served as a guide.

In the 16th and 17th centuries, Italian missionaries came to the area that is now the American Southwest. Father Eusebio Kino established this mission, the ruins of which still stand, in the Cocóspera valley of northern Sonora, Mexico.

Father Eusebio Kino,
Italian Jesuit priest
and missionary

Father Eusebio Kino (1645–1711) was another early Italian missionary. From 1681 until his death, the priest established at least 24 missions in northwestern Mexico and Arizona. He preached to the native people and gave them food and cattle. Several of these missions have become the sites of modern towns and cities. Kino also explored and mapped the Colorado River and traveled to the Pacific coast of California. Father Eusebio gained fame for drawing a map that showed southern California as part of the continent and not an island as most Europeans believed.

The Colonists

Apart from the explorers and missionaries, a few skilled workers came to America from Italy in the 17th century. Early records of the English colonies show Italian-named musicians, sculptors, glassblowers, wine merchants, and teachers scattered among the early colonists. Some were immigrants, while others visited for a short time to experience the culture of the region. Unfortunately, we know very little about these people.

One Italian colonist we know a lot about is Philip (Filippo) Mazzei. When he came to America in 1773, he began experimental farming near Thomas Jefferson's plantation in Virginia. Mazzei grew grapes and olives –crops native to Italy–and cultivated friendships with many colonial leaders. Mazzei was a freethinker whose ideas were more radical than most of the other colonists. He believed strongly in religious freedom, and he believed that the English colonies could not be a true democracy while being dominated by England. Many colonial leaders listened closely to him, especially Jefferson. Ideas Mazzei expressed in a series of articles were echoed by the authors of the Constitution of the United States.

Philip Mazzei

Another Italian who shaped early American history was Guiseppe Vigo. In the years before the Revolutionary War, Vigo became the wealthiest fur trader on the western frontier. When the war broke out against England in 1775, he joined the American rebels. He gave his financial support to George Rogers Clark, a soldier who was attempting to win the territory west of the Appalachian mountains from the British. When Clark planned to take the city of Vincennes, now in Indiana, he asked Guiseppe Vigo to scout the city. Convincing the British that he was only a fur trader and neutral in the struggle, Vigo was able to enter the city and estimate the strength of the British force there. He also discovered that the people of the city were on the colonists' side. With Vigo's help, Clark's forces took the city from the British and won the land for the rebels.

Giacomo Beltrami was an Italian-American settler of a slightly later date. He came to the United States in 1822, went west, and explored the Minnesota territory. Beltrami is credited by some authorities as being the first European to reach the source of the Mississippi River.

Giacomo Beltrami

Political Exiles

The navigators, the missionaries, and the early colonists were adventurers. But some Italian immigrants were political fugitives. They were exiled from Italy because of their participation in illegal organizations or because of their part in failed revolutions.

At the beginning of the 19th century, Italy was divided into many small states governed by foreign rulers, many from Austria. Italians objected to the foreign rule and hoped for reform. In the 1820s and 1830s, Italian patriots fought to expel the foreign rulers and unify the country. The revolts were unsuccessful.

With each failed revolt, the revolutionaries went into exile to avoid being jailed. Many of them came to the United States. A small colony of Italians developed in New York City. There the exiles established the first Italian-American newspaper, *L'Eco d'Italia,* to keep up with events in their homeland. They also set up the Italian Guard, a military organization to train young men for the continuing struggle in Italy.

In the early 19th century, Italian revolutionaries fought to end foreign rule of Italy.

The flow of Italian patriots to America was especially heavy after the failure of a great uprising in 1848. Many of the exiles served in the U.S. Army during the Civil War (1861–1865). It is estimated that more than 200 Italian Americans served as officers. One of them, L. W. Tinelli, organized a regiment of foreign-born soldiers. He named it the Garibaldi Guard, in honor of the famous Italian revolutionary, Giuseppe Garibaldi, who lived for a time in New York as an exile. The regiment had a distinguished war record. It fought at the battles of Bull Run, Harper's Ferry, and Gettysburg and was present when General Grant received General Lee's surrender.

Italy was finally united in 1861, after wars drove out the foreign rulers and Garibaldi's troops captured southern Italy and the city of Naples. By this time, many Italians had left—the United States among their destinations. Between 1820 and 1865, approximately 17,000 Italians entered North America.

The Garibaldi Guard was an Italian-American regiment of the U.S. Army that fought in the Civil War.

2
MASS IMMIGRATION

The Industrial Revolution

During the last years of the 19th century and the first decades of the 20th, the United States underwent a momentous change. During this period, people developed new sources of power, such as natural gas and electricity. Industrials built hundreds of factories filled with power-driven machines.

As late as 1890, the United States was primarily an agricultural country, with 42 percent of its labor force in farming. At the close of the century, however, the focus of the American economy began to shift rapidly to industry. The new American factories and mills needed more and more workers. States and private companies sent agents to Italy and other European countries, promising good jobs to anyone who would come to the United States.

Up to this point, the Italian government had discouraged the emigration of its citizens. The rulers felt that emigration would rob Italy of talents needed at home. During the last quarter of the 19th century, however, Italy's population grew tremendously. Between 1871 and 1905, it increased by 25 percent. The Italian government came to see emigration as a way of relieving overcrowding, and it removed most restrictions on emigration.

Not all Italians wanted to leave their homeland, however. The northern part of Italy was undergoing industrial growth, just as in the United States. Few northerners emigrated to America. They found jobs in Italian factories instead. But southern Italy, in Calbria, Naples, and the island of Sicily, remained

Immigrants on an Atlantic liner, 1906. Many Italians were brought to the United States by labor contractors, called padrones, who often advanced passage money to whole shiploads of potential workers.

Most Italian immigrants came from the south of Italy.

agricultural. Hard luck came to these southern farmers in a series of natural disasters—droughts, earthquakes, volcanic eruptions, and plant parasites. A particular parasite that attacked southern Italy's vineyards almost completely destroyed the area's wine industry in the 1890s. Thousands of people lived in poverty in the south. They were eager for a new beginning, and they saw promise in the United States.

Immigration and Quotas

The first two decades of the 20th century were the great years of Italian immigration. Although the number of arrivals had been increasing steadily since the 1880s, the pace of immigration quickened after the turn of the century. Between 1901 and 1920, more than 3 million Italians entered the United States.

This massive influx of Italians and other new immigrant groups caused resentment among many of the less-recent immigrants, especially after World War I (1914–1918). Many people felt that Italian Americans were taking jobs away from people who had been in the United States for many years. In 1921 and 1924, Congress set limits on European immigration. It set annual immigration quotas for each country, based on the numbers of each nationality already living in the United States. For every 100 Italians living in the United States, for example, only two Italian people were allowed to immigrate.

Italian immigration declined steadily throughout the next several decades. Under the quota system, only about 5,000 Italians were allowed to enter the country each year. Italians had already made a huge impact on the country, however. Between 1890 and 1950, more than 4,700,000 Italians immigrated to the United States. The census of 1940 showed that the 4,594,780 Italian Americans made up 13 percent of the country's population of people who were foreign-born or had a foreign-born parent. Italian Americans were the second largest ethnic group, exceeded only slightly by German Americans.

For every 100 Italians living in the United States, only two Italian people were allowed to immigrate.

Areas of Settlement

A move to the United States usually involved a complete change in the Italian immigrant's way of life. Newcomers to the United States had once been able to find cheap, or even free, land to farm in the country's western territories. By the close of the 19th century, when the Italians began to come in significant numbers, the frontier was gone and the free land virtually all taken up.

A few Italians were able to find agricultural work in the United States. They established farms in New England, the Great Lakes region, and Florida and grew fruits and vegetables. Other Italian immigrants grew grapes and founded vineyards in California.

Italian immigrants at work pressing grapes for wine in a California vineyard

Some Sicilians found a place for themselves in the fishing industries on the Gulf and Pacific coasts. In San Francisco, Italian immigrants found work on the wharfs and boats. Only a small fraction of Italian immigrants were able to work in jobs they had at home, however. The immigrants were most often brought over by labor contractors, who found them jobs in industry.

Many of the early immigrants intended to stay in America only for a short time. They planned to work hard, save their money, and then return to their villages and purchase land. Through the first decade of the 20th century, thousands of immigrants left the United States each year to return to Italy. In 1908, for example, 160,000 sailed back home. This was about half the number of Italians who entered the United States that year.

Soon, though, Italian immigrants began to think of America as a new and permanent home. Men who had left their wives and children behind in Italy saved their earnings for their family's passage to the United States. They made homes for themselves in the industrial cities of the Northeast. They were loyal to their work, becoming active in labor unions. They often joined existing unions or organized new ones in the stone, garment, and building industries.

Italian families came to New York, Boston, and other cities where factories offered work. The 1940 census found that 88 percent of Italian Americans lived in cities. They became significant minorities in Connecticut, Massachusetts, New Jersey, New York, Pennsylvania, and Rhode Island. By 1930, New York City had more than 1 million Italian Americans. Smaller groups of Italian Americans settled elsewhere, such as in California, Colorado, Delaware, Illinois, Nevada, and Ohio.

Italian-American women and children often worked out of the family home. Here a family sews for a clothing business in the early 1900s.

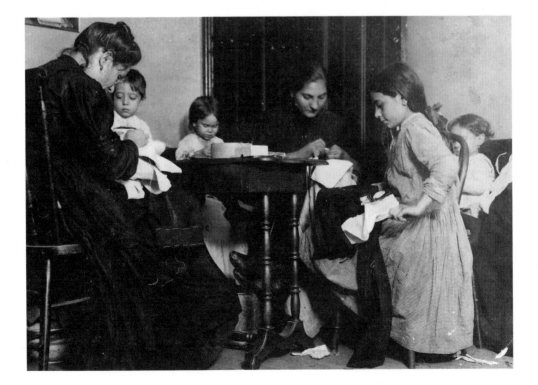

3
LIFE IN THE UNITED STATES

Little Italys

Some Italian immigrants did not find permanent homes in the United States. They wandered from town to town in search of work. They joined crews building railroads, mixing cement, and laying highways. They helped to construct the new tall buildings that were filling out city skylines and to dig the new subways. These workers were forced to move every few months, and they had little opportunity to put down roots.

Many immigrant families were attracted to the American industrial centers, however. Cities often came to have a "Little Italy," a neighborhood inhabited almost entirely by Italian Americans. The cities with the largest Italian-American populations all had Little Italys—New York, Philadelphia, Chicago, Boston, and New Haven, Connecticut, among them.

Little Italys allowed Italian Americans to retain their cultural identity. Spoken Italian, familiar foods, street music, Italian theater and opera, Italian churches and celebrations were all a part of life in a Little Italy. Often a Little Italy was divided into sections, each occupied by immigrants from the same village or district in their native Italy. Sicilians lived on one

Mulberry Street, on the Lower East Side of New York City, ran through the heart of New York's Little Italy.

block, Neapolitans on another. Familiar faces and customs were comforting to new immigrants who felt they didn't fit in with the rest of American culture. Little Italys made the Italian immigrants feel protected, as if they had brought their hometowns with them overseas.

Italian immigrants were also drawn to these neighborhoods by low rents. Little Italys developed in areas of the city where earlier immigrant groups, such as Irish and Germans, had once lived. Italians occupied tenements—low-cost apartment houses built for poor immigrants—which had long since seen their best days. Most were unheated, and many did not have indoor bathrooms. The buildings were sometimes crumbling and always overcrowded. Families of five or six people often crowded into one tiny room. Sickness and disease raged through the Italian immigrant community.

Prejudice and Discrimination

The majority of Americans—everyone but Native Americans—are descendants of immigrants. The first immigrants were from northern and western Europe. They became the ruling majority in the early United States. To these people, the Italian immigrant culture was very foreign.

Looking at housing conditions in Italian-American neighborhoods, many people concluded that the immigrants must be inferior. Because many Italian Americans worked as unskilled laborers, people thought they could do no other work. Italian immigrants tended to settle disputes among themselves rather than turn to the police. Rumors circulated of the violence and lawlessness of Italians. Actually, statistics show that the Italian-American crime rate

Outside an Italian grocery shop in New York's Little Italy, about 1890

was not significantly different from the national average, and it was even lower than that of most other immigrant groups.

Nicola Sacco and Bartolomeo Vanzetti

The unreasonable prejudice against Italians reached hysteria in 1891, when more than 100 Italian men were arrested for killing a police officer in New Orleans. Ten of these men, who were tried and found not guilty or were still awaiting trial, were lynched by a mob. An 11th Italian man was also killed by the mob, pulled from jail where he was serving a sentence for an unrelated minor crime.

In the 1920s, another famous case brought to light the prejudice against Italian Americans. Nicola Sacco and Bartolomeo Vanzetti were convicted of murder with scanty evidence. They were electrocuted in 1927, after seven years of denied appeals. The men's names were not cleared until 1978, when Massachusetts governor Michael Dukakis signed a proclamation declaring a memorial day for Sacco and Vanzetti. A report by the governor's legal counsel stated that with the deaths of Sacco and Vanzetti, it was possible that "a grievous miscarriage of justice occurred."

The violent image of Italian Americans was fueled by rumors of their connections with the Mafia crime organization, which began in Italy. And because of their involvement in labor unions, Italian Americans were often unfairly blamed for the violence that accompanied labor disputes in the early 20th century.

Forced to live in the most rundown sections of the city, and faced with the hostility of other ethnic groups, many immigrants lost heart and chose to return to Italy. Most, however, kept their faith in America.

Many immigrants lost heart and chose to return to Italy.

Helping Each Other

Social workers and reformers worked to improve conditions in Little Italys. They came from both within and outside the Italian-American community. Mother Cabrini, a nun well known for her work with immigrants, came from Italy to help the cause.

Maria Francesca Cabrini (1850–1917) had from an early age dreamed of doing missionary work for the Catholic church. She trained to be a schoolteacher, and in 1880 she founded the Missionary Sisters of the Sacred Heart, hoping to teach poor children in China and India. Pope Leo XIII, however, convinced Mother Cabrini that there was important work to be done among Italian immigrants in the United States. Bringing her followers with her, she worked in Chicago and New York, opening schools, orphanages, and hospitals for immigrants. Mother Cabrini was declared a saint by the Roman Catholic church in 1946, the first U.S. citizen to be so honored.

After gaining a foothold in their new country, Italian Americans also learned how to help themselves. Italian-owned banks provided immigrants with money they needed to start businesses when no other banks would. Legal agencies and hundreds of mutual aid

societies helped the Italian-American community grow. Italian Americans established their own self-help organizations. The largest of these was the *Ordine Figli d'Italia*—the Order of the Sons of Italy. This organization, founded in 1904, had at its height more than 300,000 members nationwide. It created summer camps for children and nursing homes for older members of the community. In its early days, the Sons of Italy conducted English language classes for the new immigrants who wanted to become more "American." In later years, it established Italian language schools for the members of the second and third generations who wanted to learn more about their heritage.

Italian Americans also established their own newspapers and journals. The pioneering paper was *L'Eco d'Italia*, founded in 1849. New newspapers and magazines emerged, all very popular with the immigrant community. The papers gave assistance and advice, they listed jobs, and they covered news from Italy. By the 1930s, the Italian press held second place in circulation among the foreign language newspapers in New York City.

Left: Mother Francesca Cabrini, an Italian missionary to the United States who was named a saint by the Roman Catholic church

Right: One of the many hospitals established by Mother Cabrini, New York City's Cabrini Medical Center, as it looks today

Gaining Ground

As the 20th century progressed, Italian Americans moved into all sectors of the U.S. job market. When they first came to the United States, few Italian immigrants spoke English. But in time they learned the language and customs of the United States and were able to qualify for a variety of jobs. In 1916 almost half of all Italian Americans were unskilled laborers. By 1931 only 30 percent were still in this category. In subsequent years this figure declined further until the census of 1950 showed only 11 percent working in unskilled jobs.

Italian Americans became mechanics, plasterers, bakers, and butchers. Many turned to barbering. At one point, about 85 percent of New York's barbers were of Italian descent. Large numbers of Italian Americans became skilled workers in the cloth trades.

A New York City barber shop, around 1900

At one time, the Italians all but monopolized the garment industry in Philadelphia. Almost a third of the garment workers in Chicago, Boston, and New York were of Italian origin. Italian Americans became equally numerous in the textile industry of New England.

In recognition of Italian-American women's important place in the industry, the International Ladies' Garment Workers Union (ILGWU) chartered an Italian-speaking chapter in 1919. The general secretary of Local 89, which enrolled 37,000 members, was Luigi Antonioni. He was also the first vice-president of the ILGWU, and he organized an Italian-American labor council with a membership of over 300,000.

Other Italians became business professionals, store clerks, and merchants. Children of immigrants began attending colleges and universities. In increasing numbers, they entered managerial positions. By 1950 Italian Americans were distributed through the job market in roughly the same proportions as the rest of the U.S. population.

Italian-American stone carvers lend their skill to sculptures for the Wisconsin State Capitol building in Madison, Wisconsin, 1911.

World War II

The absorption of Italian immigrants into mainstream America was demonstrated by their loyalty during World War II (1939-1945). When the dictator Benito Mussolini first came to power in Italy, some Italian Americans championed his Fascist government. Under Mussolini, the Fascist Party reduced unemployment and brought economic growth to Italy. But other Italian Americans were firm opponents of Fascism, and they condemned the criminal acts of Mussolini's government.

When the United States declared war on Italy in 1941, the most prominent Italian-American newspapers rejected Fascism and whole-heartedly supported the U.S. government's war effort. More than 400,000 Italian Americans served the United States during World War II. They distinguished themselves in every branch of the armed services, and at least seven received the Congressional Medal of Honor. Ironically, the war in Italy offered many second-generation Italian Americans their first opportunity to see the towns and villages of their parents.

During World War II, many Italian Americans protested Mussolini's Fascist government.

Two American sergeants look on as a native Italian shoemaker cobbles shoes in Italy during World War II.

Al Pacino, left, and Marlon Brando star in The Godfather, *a very popular film of the 1970s about an Italian Mafia family. Many Italian Americans were concerned that the film promoted the stereotype of Italian Americans as gangsters.*

Shaking Stereotypes

Despite the progress they have made, Italian Americans are still burdened by unfortunate stereotypes. Gangsterism in America has become associated with Italian Americans, and the stereotypical Italian American of the media, critics claim, is shown either singing, cooking, or killing.

To most Americans in the 1990s, organized crime equals the Mafia, and the Mafia is composed of Italian Americans. This secret criminal organization did develop in Italy. But organized crime is a multiethnic enterprise that has no more to do with Italians than anyone else. According to the Federal Bureau of Investigation (FBI), 500,000 people are involved in organized crime. Perhaps 20,000 of these are associates of the Mafia network, and of these, 1,700—fewer than 10 percent—are of Italian-American background.

All the same, movies, books, and even newspapers perpetuate the Mafia myth. Films such as *The Godfather, Prizzi's Honor,* and *Wise Guys,* and television shows such as "The Untouchables," with their Italian-American Mafia characters, ensure that the Mafia image remains popular. The Mafia stereotype is not likely to go away soon, because of American society's fascination with stories of crime and violence. Italian Americans are hopeful that the stereotyping eventually will be overwhelmed, however, by the promotion of more positive and authentic images.

President Jimmy Carter signs a document proclaiming Italian-American Heritage Week in New York City, October 14, 1980. New York Congresswoman Geraldine Ferraro looks on.

The 2000-seat opera house of the Brooklyn Academy of Music, Brooklyn, New York, was built in 1908. Its design was based on the traditional Italian opera house.

4
CONTRIBUTIONS TO AMERICAN LIFE

Business and Industry

Italian immigrants and the generations that followed them have made important contributions to life in the United States. Many Italian Americans found success in business and industry.

Amadeo Giannini (1870–1949) was the son of immigrants who had come to California. At the age of 12, Amadeo went to work for a produce firm. By 19 he had become a partner in the business. At age 30 he opened a small bank in San Francisco and specialized in making loans to people of limited means who could not usually find credit. By 1930 he had built this small bank into the powerful Bank of America, with branch offices from coast to coast.

John F. Cuneo of Chicago began a book bindery business in 1907, and in 1919 he expanded into printing. The Cuneo Press printed many U.S. magazines with circulations in the millions. Eventually the Cuneo Press became the largest printing company in the world, with plants in San Francisco, Chicago, Milwaukee, Philadelphia, and New York.

Italian Americans have been especially successful in the food businesses. Marco Fontana, for example, founded the California Fruit Packing Corporation in 1889. Later called Del Monte, the company became the largest producer of canned fruits and vegetables in the world.

When chef Hector Boiardi was 17, he immigrated to the United States and worked a series of jobs as a hotel cook. In 1924 he started his own restaurant in Cleveland, Ohio. His special spaghetti and sauce became so popular that he soon opened a packaged food business, the Chef Boiardi Food Products Company. As the company grew, Boiardi opened a large factory in Pennsylvania and renamed the product Chef Boyardee. Boiardi's canned pastas fed the U.S. troops and their allies during World War II, and Chef Boyardee and Spaghetti-Os became household words.

Amedeo Obici is another business leader who started small. In 1897 he rented some sidewalk space, built a small stand out of wood, and bought a peanut roaster for $4.50. Obici teamed up with partner M. M. Peruzzi, and their peanut company, now called Planters, was incorporated in 1906. In 1917 Obici invented Mr. Peanut for the company's first national ad campaign. Through the years, Planters Peanut Company has become a leading producer of peanuts, peanut butter, and candy in the United States.

Domenico Ghirardelli

Chocolatier Domenico Ghirardelli, born in Italy, first took his chocolate manufacturing business to Peru. Then he heard that gold had been discovered in the United States, and he joined the 1849 gold rush to California. He eventually settled in San Francisco, where he again took up making chocolate and other sweets. By the 1870s and 1880s, Ghirardelli was selling several million pounds of chocolate each year. The D. Ghirardelli Company of San Francisco is still one of the largest chocolate manufacturers in the United States.

It was an Italian American, Jeno Paulucci, of Hibbing, Minnesota, who began Chun King Foods, a leading processor of Chinese food. Paulucci sold the business to R. J. Reynolds Industries for $60 million. Paulucci then started a Duluth frozen pizza business, Jeno's, which he eventually sold to Pillsbury Co. for about $200 million. Then, in the late 1980s, Paulucci launched a chain of Pizza Kwik pizza delivery shops.

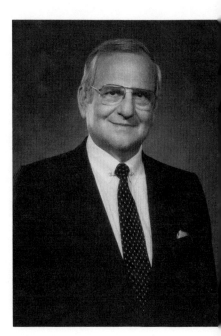

Lee Iacocca

Considering Italy's reputation as one of the greatest wine-producing countries, it's not surprising that Italian Americans have bottled some very popular wines. Ernest and Julio Gallo's father started the family vineyard in Modesto, California. When he died, Ernest and Julio decided to switch from growing grapes to making wine. They initially sold wine in bulk to bottlers, but in 1938 they started doing their own bottling under the Gallo label. Decade by decade sales grew, and a major advertising campaign of the late 1980s made Gallo wine a best-seller.

Auto executive Lee Iacocca is an Italian American of tremendous celebrity. His autobiography *Iacocca* (1984) sold more than six-and-a-half million copies. In a 1985 poll, Americans rated Lee Iacocca the third most respected person in the world, only after President Ronald Reagan and Pope John Paul II. Iacocca became president of Ford Motor Company in 1970, and president and chief executive officer of Chrysler Corporation in 1978. By cutting waste and costs, Iacocca turned the financially troubled company around.

New York Mayor Fiorello La Guardia speaking at a Columbus Day celebration in 1942

Politics

The first Italian American to achieve national prominence was Fiorello La Guardia (1882–1947). Affectionately known as the "Little Flower," he was one of the most colorful and beloved figures on the American political scene. He began his political career as deputy attorney of the state of New York, and then won election to Congress on the Republican ticket— the first Italian American to do so. When the United States entered World War I the year after his election, La Guardia volunteered for the Army Air Corps. Serving on the Italian front, he quickly rose to the rank of major and was decorated by King Victor Emmanuel of Italy. In 1918, while he was still in military service, La Guardia's district again returned him to the House of Representatives. Holding a Congressional seat almost continuously until 1932, La Guardia attracted national attention with his campaign to improve the conditions of workers.

Although he lost his Congressional seat in a 1932 Democratic landslide, La Guardia quickly bounded back. The following year, he was elected mayor of New York City, breaking the longtime hold of Democrats on the city. He was reelected in 1937 and 1941. As mayor, La Guardia endeared himself to the voters. Perhaps his most important contribution was a program to tear down the city's slums and replace the tenements with new, low-cost housing.

John O. Pastore was the first Italian American to serve as the governor of a state, occupying that office in Rhode Island from 1945 to 1950. He then was elected to the United States Senate, where he served until 1977.

John A. Volpe was elected governor of Massachusetts in 1964, and, five years later, he became U.S. Secretary of Transportation under President Richard Nixon. In 1972, Volpe was named U.S. ambassador to Italy. Ella Tambussi Grasso (1919–1981), served two terms in the U.S. Congress, then was elected governor of Connecticut in 1974. Grasso was the first woman in the country to be elected governor. She was reelected in 1979, but resigned a year later because of illness.

Starting his career as a lawyer in a Brooklyn law firm, Mario Cuomo gained public recognition for his representation of community groups in the 1960s. In 1974 governor Hugh Carey appointed Cuomo New York's secretary of state, and in 1978 Cuomo was elected lieutenant governor as Carey's running mate. Cuomo ran for governor of the state in 1982, defeating New York mayor Ed Koch in the primary and his Republican opponent that November. New York reelected Governor Cuomo in 1986 and 1990.

Geraldine Ferraro was the first and only woman to run for vice-president of the United States. She was on the ticket with Democratic presidential candidate Walter Mondale in 1984. Ferraro had been an assistant district attorney of Queens, New York, and a member of Congress from New York from 1980 to 1984. Mondale and Ferraro were defeated by their Republican opponents, Ronald Reagan and George Bush.

Mario Cuomo

Geraldine Ferraro

U.S. Supreme Court justice Antonin Scalia

When President Ronald Reagan appointed Antonin Scalia to the Supreme Court in 1986, Scalia became the first Italian-American Supreme Court justice. On the road to the Supreme Court, Scalia attended Harvard Law School, was a law professor at the University of Chicago, and served on the United States Court of Appeals for the District of Columbia. The conservative Scalia was the youngest of the justices when appointed to the Supreme Court at age 50.

Art and Music

Artist Constantino Brumaldi heads the list of Italian Americans who have distinguished themselves in art. As a young man, Brumaldi was an active Italian patriot and took part in the uprisings that swept Italy in 1848. After the revolution failed, Brumaldi came to the United States, where he contributed his talents to the decoration of the Capitol in Washington, D.C.

He designed and painted a series of murals that illustrate U.S. history, and he began to paint a huge frieze around the great central rotunda of the Capitol. Brumaldi died before finishing the work, but a student of his completed the painting.

Luigi Palmi di Cesnola, after immigrating to the United States, served as a major in the 11th New York Cavalry during the Civil War. In reward for his service, Cesnola was named by President Lincoln to be the American consul on Cyprus. While at this diplomatic post, Cesnola became interested in the excavation of the historical monuments of the island. Although he had no formal training in archaeology and only limited funds, he was able to recover thousands of relics of an ancient Mediterranean civilization. The New York Metropolitan Museum agreed to take and maintain the whole collection. Soon after this, Cesnola became the secretary and then the director of the newly opened Metropolitan. Cesnola served as director from 1879 until his death in 1904 and was instrumental in building up the museum's collections and establishing its international reputation.

Harry Bertoia (1915–1978) was an Italian-American sculptor who, after World War II, began to adapt the techniques of industrial metalwork to fine art. He created many sculptures for public buildings. One of his best known works, called *Golden Screen,* is displayed at the Manufacturer's Trust Bank in New York City. The sculptured bronze screen stands 15 feet high and is 70 feet long. Its 800 panels are held together by an intricate web of steel bars. Bertoia was also a noted designer of jewelry and furniture. His famous "wire chair" won him numerous awards.

Italian immigrant Simon Rodia held various jobs as a construction worker and a tile setter throughout his life. He was also an artist with a unique vision. In 1921 Rodia purchased a triangle-shaped lot in South Central Los Angeles and began work on the masterpiece of his lifetime, which he called *Nuestro Pueblo,* ("Our Town"). Over a period of 33 years, Rodia built

Harry Bertoia poses with his sculpture Sunlit Straw *in Minneapolis, Minnesota.*

Sculptor Simon Rodia at work on his masterpiece, Nuestro Pueblo, *in South Central Los Angeles. The immigrant Rodia worked daily on his sculpture for 33 years, from 1921 to 1953, and became a well-known figure in this Los Angeles community.*

the nine connecting sculptures from structural steel and mortar. In the mortar, Rodia set seashells, bits of broken glass and pottery, and broken tiles that he saved from his day jobs as a tile setter. The tallest sculpture, or tower, stands 99.5 feet tall. The monument also features a gazebo with a circular bench and several bird baths, and it is surrounded by a wall adorned with mosaics of tile and glass. The Watts Towers of Simon Rodia are now recognized as a monument to the human spirit and are a California Historic Monument and a Historic Park.

Artist Frank Stella is widely recognized as one of the most accomplished abstract painters of the 20th century. In the late 1950s, Stella won renown for a group of "pinstripe" paintings—paintings of black parallel bands on bare canvas. The excitement surrounding these paintings helped launch minimalism, a popular avant-garde style of the 1960s. Stella's later work is marked by very bright metallic or fluorescent colors. Collections of Stella's paintings are displayed in dozens of museums around the world.

Frank Stella

Of all the gifts Italians have brought to American culture, opera is one of the most treasured. Enrico Caruso, the internationally famous tenor born in Naples, Italy, had a brilliant career with the Metropolitan Opera in the early 1900s. His repertoire included 43 operas. Opera composer Gian Carlo Menotti is the 20th century composer whose work is most often performed. His *Amahl and the Night Visitors* (1951), an opera that tells the story of a poor crippled boy who meets the Three Kings on their way to Bethlehem, is now a Christmas standard.

Cellist Arturo Toscanini (1867–1957) became one of the most celebrated conductors of recent times. Toscanini conducted at the Metropolitan Opera from 1908 to 1915, and from 1926 to 1936 he headed the New York Philharmonic Orchestra. In the 1930s, Toscanini began a memorable series of radio broadcasts, bringing music into the homes of millions of

Enrico Caruso made his American debut with the Metropolitan Opera in 1903 and was a star of that company until his death in 1920.

Arturo Toscanini

Americans. Because of the immense popularity of these broadcasts, the National Broadcasting Company created a symphony orchestra specifically for the great conductor. Toscanini headed this NBC Symphony from its beginnings in 1937 until his retirement in 1954.

Henry Mancini, born in 1924, took his first music lessons from his father, who played in a Sons of Italy band. The composer, arranger, and conductor won Oscars for the musical scores from *Breakfast at Tiffany's* and *Days of Wine and Roses,* and more than 20 Grammy awards for his popular songs. He is probably best known for the song "Moon River," from *Breakfast at Tiffany's,* as well as the "Pink Panther Theme."

Scholarship, Science, and Literature

Italian Americans have taught at leading U.S. colleges and universities from the schools' earliest days. Lorenzo da Ponte, a poet, worked in Europe writing librettos (texts) for Mozart's operas. After coming to the United States in 1805, da Ponte started the study of Italian at Columbia University in New York City.

Gaetano Salvemini (1873–1957), a noted historian of the French Revolution, began his career at several universities in Italy. Entering politics, he won election to the Italian Parliament, where he was an outspoken enemy of Fascism. After being imprisoned for his views, Professor Salvemini went into exile, and he eventually joined the faculty of Harvard University, where he lectured from 1934 to 1948.

Enrico Fermi (1901–1954), born in Italy, was also an exile from Mussolini's regime. Fermi taught at the universities of Florence and Rome, and in 1938 he was awarded the Nobel Prize for physics for his work with artificial radioactivity. An opponent of the Fascists, Fermi fled Italy via a trip to Sweden to accept the Nobel Prize. After coming to the United States, Fermi became a professor at Columbia University and then at the University of Chicago. Fermi experimented with uranium fission (the splitting of uranium atoms), and along with Leo Lziliard, an immigrant from Hungary, Fermi conducted the first controlled nuclear reaction. This experiment of 1942 led directly to the development of the atomic bomb.

Left: Enrico Fermi
Right: Emilio Segre

Emilio Segre (1905–1989) was an associate of Fermi's at the University of Rome. In 1936 Segre discovered technicium, the first element to be artificially created. After coming to the United States in 1938, Professor Segre joined the staff of the Lawrence Radiation Laboratory at the University of California at Berkeley. During World War II, he was a member of the Los Alamos Scientific Laboratory, where the first atomic bomb was produced. Returning to Berkeley after the war, Dr. Segre discovered the antiproton, a key to understanding nuclear physics. Segre received the Nobel Prize for physics in 1959 for this important discovery.

Mario Pei (1901–1978) taught linguistics, the science of language, at Columbia University from 1937 to 1970. Through more than 20 books he brought the study of linguistics and word origins to a wide readership. Pei wrote the acclaimed companion works *The Story of Language* (1949) and *The Story of English* (1952).

A. Bartlett Giamatti (1938–1989) taught English and literature at Yale University for two decades, beginning in 1966. He became president of Yale, a position he held from 1978 to 1986. He then became president of baseball's National League in 1986 and the commissioner of baseball in April 1989, a position he held until his death later that year.

Author and literary critic Bernard De Voto (1897–1955) began his career as a teacher at Northwestern and Harvard universities, but soon turned to writing. From 1936 to 1938, he was editor of the *Saturday Review of Literature,* and he edited for *Harper's Magazine* for the last 20 years of his life. He wrote many books on American literature and social history, biographical and critical studies, and fiction, including mystery stories under the pen name John August. *Across the Wide Missouri,* in which De Voto tells the story of the pioneers of the American West, was awarded the 1948 Pulitzer Prize in history.

Writer Paul Gallico (1897–1976) worked for 13 years on the staff of the *New York Daily News* as movie critic, sportswriter, editor, and columnist. Leaving the paper in 1936, he became a free-lance fiction

A. Bartlett Giamatti

writer. He wrote for leading magazines and newspapers and published 41 books. During World War II, he was the European correspondent for *Cosmopolitan*. Gallico also wrote children's stories, fables, ghost stories, and screenplays.

Poet John Ciardi (1916–1986) published more than 40 volumes of poetry, essays, and books in his lifetime. He taught for many years at Rutgers and Harvard universities and served as the poetry editor of the magazine *Saturday Review* from 1956 to 1972. Ciardi is probably best known for his book *How Does a Poem Mean?* (1959) and his translations of the Italian poet Dante, which have received international acclaim.

Evan Hunter wrote his first book, *The Blackboard Jungle* (1954), about delinquency in schools, after several difficult months teaching English in a New York City high school. Since then he has written more than 70 novels, many of them hard-boiled detective stories under the pen name Ed McBain. Born Salvatore Lambino in Manhattan, New York, he changed his name to Evan Hunter because he felt many people held a bias against writers with Italian names.

John Ciardi

Lawrence Ferlinghetti in front of his City Lights Bookstore, San Francisco, California

Italian-American writer Gay Talese is highly regarded for his literary nonfiction. He began his career as a feature writer at the *New York Times*. During the late 1960s, he helped to pioneer the literary movement known as "new journalism," which involves applying the techniques of fiction writing to nonfiction. Talese's best-selling books include *The Kingdom and the Power* (1969), about the *New York Times*, *Honor Thy Father* (1971), the story of a Mafia family, and *Unto the Sons* (1992), the story of Talese's own family's migration from the town of Maida in southern Italy to the United States.

Lawrence Ferlinghetti, whose father immigrated from Lombardy, Italy, was one of the leaders of the San Francisco literary scene in the 1950s. He was part of the "Beat Generation" of avant-garde writers. Ferlinghetti helped the Beat movement grow as the owner of City Lights, a San Francisco bookstore and small press. He is also a poet, novelist, playwright, and painter. A book of Ferlinghetti's poetry published in 1958, called *A Coney Island of the Mind*, has gone through 28 printings and has sold almost 700,000 copies in the United States alone. With more than 1 million copies sold in other countries, *A Coney Island of the Mind* is the largest-selling single book by a living American poet.

Entertainment

Countless Italian Americans have excelled in the entertainment industry, from popular musicians to film stars. Through the years, Americans have danced to the bands of Ted Fiorito, Vincent Rose, Tony Pastor, Louis Prima, Ralph Marterie, and Guy Lombardo, leader of the well-known "Royal Canadians." Teenagers in the 1950s swung to the Italian-American doo-wop bands. And before rock 'n' roll, the heavyweights of popular music were all Italian-American.

Singer Dean Martin was born Dino Crocetti in 1917. His career took off in film when he teamed up with comic Jerry Lewis. Lewis clowned and mugged while Martin sang and played the straight man. Together Martin and Lewis made 16 movies. After the act broke up, Martin took his songs to his own television variety show on NBC and was a popular nightclub performer for many years.

Frank Sinatra

Frank Sinatra started his career in 1939, singing with trombonist Tommy Dorsey and his band. Sinatra claims he picked up his distinctive singing style, characterized by pausing, phrasing, and *glissando* (sliding up or down the notes of a scale) from Tommy Dorsey—he learned to imitate the way Dorsey phrased with his trombone. Sinatra left Dorsey's band in 1942 to become a soloist, and he immediately became a teen idol. By the 1960s, he was one of the biggest show-business attractions of the 20th century. Sinatra made dozens of recordings and starred in two television shows in the 1950s. He also appeared in many films, including *Anchors Aweigh* (1945), *Guys and Dolls* (1955), and *High Society* (1956). He won the best supporting actor Oscar in 1953 for his part in *From Here to Eternity*.

Tony Bennett, another popular singer of the 1940s, was born Anthony Dominick Benedetto in Queens, New York. His best-known song, "I Left My Heart in San Francisco," sold more than 1.5 million copies in 1962. Tony Bennett has sold more records than any other vocalist of his generation.

Tony Bennett

Madonna

A true pop phenomenon of the 1980s and 1990s, Madonna has probably made a bigger worldwide impact than any other single entertainer. Her hard-driving dance music and elaborate stage shows have sold out concerts across the globe. A style-maker and a trendsetter, her records have sold millions of copies each, and she has starred in several hit movies. Madonna was born Madonna Ciccone in Bay City, Michigan.

Another area of entertainment dominated by Italian Americans is the film industry. The director Francis Ford Coppola's films include such blockbusters as *The Godfather* (1972) and its two sequels, and the Vietnam War story *Apocalypse Now* (1979). *The Godfather,* which Coppola also cowrote with Mario

Puzo, won Oscars for best picture and best adapted screenplay. Coppola has also directed such popular films as *The Outsiders* (1983) and *Peggy Sue Got Married* (1986).

Martin Scorsese has a controversial, realistic style of filmmaking that is characterized by the theme of the "outsider." Many of Scorsese's films may have suffered at the box office because of their grim subject matter and their violence, but the same films have been praised by critics. Scorsese's *Taxi Driver* won the grand prize at the Cannes Film Festival in 1976, and *Raging Bull* (1980) has been called one of the best American films ever made. *GoodFellas* (1990) was another critical success for Scorsese.

Director Brian DePalma is often named as the heir to Alfred Hitchcock's title, "Master of the Macabre." Best known for his technically dazzling films such as *Carrie* (1976) and *Blow Out* (1981), DePalma feels that suspense and horror films are important as well as entertaining, because of their emphasis on purely visual storytelling.

Francis Ford Coppola

Martin Scorsese

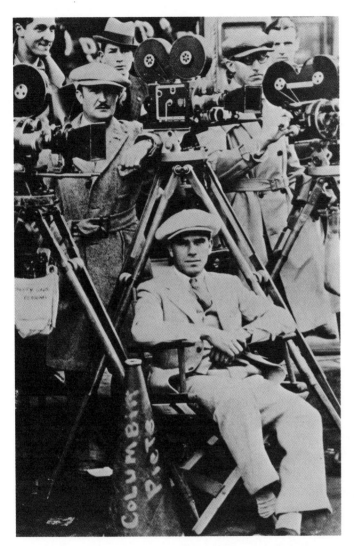

Frank Capra

Also among Hollywood's most respected directors are Frank Capra and Vincente Minnelli. Capra's long list of now-classic films includes *It Happened One Night* (1934), *Meet John Doe* (1941), *Arsenic and Old Lace* (1944), and the holiday staple *It's a Wonderful Life* (1946). His movies were idealistic, sentimental, and patriotic. Minnelli was a successful director of movie musicals such as *Meet Me in St. Louis* (1944), *An American in Paris* (1951), *The Band Wagon* (1953), and the award-winning *Gigi* (1958).

The public took notice of director Penny Marshall when her popular film *Big* (1988) became the first movie directed by a woman to take in more than $100 million at the box office. Marshall also scored hits with *Awakenings* (1990), which was nominated for three Academy Awards, including best picture, and the 1992 release *A League of Their Own*. Marshall, an Italian American who grew up in the Bronx, New York, began her career in television as Laverne De Fazio, a character in the popular 1970s sitcom "Laverne and Shirley."

Penny Marshall's brother Garry Marshall also began his entertainment career in television. He was a writer for "The Dick Van Dyke Show" and later produced the hit sitcoms "Happy Days" and "Laverne and Shirley." Then he brought his light, fast-paced sitcom style to the big screen. Marshall made *Pretty Woman* a worldwide smash hit of 1990.

Animator Joseph Barbera was born in 1911 to an Italian immigrant family in New York City, where his father owned several barber shops. When Barbera moved to California to work in the Metro-Goldwyn-Mayer studio's cartoon department, he met writer and director Bill Hanna. Together they created Tom and

Penny Marshall

Joseph Barbera, seated, with writing partner William Hanna. The Hanna-Barbera animation studio has created dozens of popular cartoon characters for television.

Jerry, the famous cartoon cat and mouse, and later they were commissioned to produce cartoons for television. At a time when most people thought animation was too time-consuming and costly to produce for television, Hanna and Barbera created new, faster animation techniques, and they turned out huge numbers of television cartoons. Some of Joe Barbera and Bill Hanna's most memorable television characters of the 1950s and 1960s are Yogi Bear, Huckleberry Hound, and Top Cat. The Hanna-Barbera studios also produced the prime-time television series "The Flintstones" and "The Jetsons," the Saturday-morning series "Scooby Doo," and the feature film *Charlotte's Web* (1973).

Many Italian Americans have had successful careers in front of the camera as well. Comedian Lou Costello (1908–1959), partner of Bud Abbott in the Abbott and Costello comedy team, began his career as a boxer and movie stuntman. Abbott and Costello brought their classic comedy routines to radio and to three dozen movies in the 1940s and 1950s.

Actress Anne Bancroft was born Annemarie Italiano in the Bronx, New York. She had appeared in 16 movies and about 90 television shows before making a strong debut on Broadway in the 1959 production of *The Miracle Worker.* Bancroft recreated her role on film and won an Oscar for her portrayal of Helen Keller's teacher, Annie Sullivan. Bancroft has starred in dozens of movies since, including *The Graduate* (1967), *Prisoner of Second Avenue* (1975), and *84 Charing Cross Road* (1987).

With the release of *Mean Streets* (1973) and *Taxi Driver* (1976), Robert de Niro was established as a star of major importance. De Niro, born in 1943 in New York City, also starred in *Raging Bull* (1980), *GoodFellas* (1990), *Awakenings* (1990), *Backdraft* (1991), and *The Godfather Part II*, for which he won a best supporting actor Oscar in 1975.

Actor Al Pacino, a New Yorker of Sicilian ancestry, began his career as a stage actor in off-Broadway and Broadway plays in the late 1960s. When he turned

Sylvester Stallone

Robert de Niro

to movies in the 1970s, he attracted the public's attention with his true-to-life roles in Francis Ford Coppola's *Godfather* films, *Serpico* (1973), and *Dog Day Afternoon* (1975). Pacino's recent projects include the films *Dick Tracy* (1990) and *Frankie and Johnny* (1991).

Sylvester Stallone, whose father was from Sicily and whose mother is French, received worldwide acclaim for the film *Rocky,* which he starred in and wrote. Stallone was nominated for best actor and best screenplay Oscars, and the film won the best picture award in 1976. Since then Stallone has starred in several sequels about the fictional fighter Rocky Balboa, as well as three films about the character of John Rambo: *First Blood, Rambo,* and *Rambo III.*

Comedian Jay Leno, whose father is Italian-American, began working as a stand-up comic to make money for college. Throughout the 1970s and 1980s, Leno performed in nightclubs and comedy clubs and on many talk shows. Johnny Carson, the host of NBC's "Tonight Show," named Leno a permanent guest host of the show in 1986. When Carson retired from the show in May 1992, Leno became the full-time host.

Rocky Marciano

Sports

Countless Italian Americans have excelled in sports, and many will be remembered in record books. Gene Sarazen was a famous golfer of the 1920s and 1930s, winning the Professional Golfers Association championship three times and the U.S. Open twice. In boxing, Lou Ambers was the lightweight champion in the 1930s, and Rocky Graziano the king of the middleweights in the late 1940s. Rocky Marciano (1923–1969), the "Brockton Bomber," was born Rocco Marchegiano. In 1952 he won the title from Jersey Joe Walcott and held it until his retirement in 1956.

In football Vince Lombardi (1913–1970) coached the Green Bay Packers to five national championships and two Super Bowl victories. At the time of his death, Lombardi was general manager, coach, and part-owner of the Washington Redskins. Joe Montana, who has played with the San Francisco 49ers since 1979, has been called the greatest quarterback of all time. Montana led the 49ers to four Super Bowl victories—in 1982, 1985, 1989, and 1990. He was named Most Valuable Player in the Super Bowl three times.

Vince Lombardi

Joe Montana

Mario Andretti was born in Trieste, Italy, in 1940 and came to the United States at the age of 15. He started automobile racing in 1964 and won the U.S. Auto Club Championship in 1965, 1966, and 1969. In 1969 he also won the Indianapolis 500. Andretti's September 1978 victory in the Italian Grand Prix won him the world driving championship in Grand Prix racing. In horse racing, Eddie Arcaro rode to five Kentucky Derby victories during the 1930s, 1940s, and 1950s. He was one of the winningest jockeys ever, with a total of 4,779 victories.

Mario Andretti

Joe DiMaggio was elected to baseball's Hall of Fame in 1955.

Dozens of Italian Americans have had outstanding careers in baseball. One of the most famous, Joe "The Clipper" DiMaggio, was a star of the New York Yankees between 1936 and 1951. The outfielder was known for his powerful hitting as well as his graceful fielding. DiMaggio was American League MVP three times and elected to several All-Star teams. Yogi Berra was a catcher for the Yankees and later managed the team. During his long career, Berra was chosen MVP three times, and he played in 14 World Series.

Mary Lou Retton

Gymnast Mary Lou Retton brought a new style to her sport, and she became known for her power and speed. When Retton won a gold, two silver, and two bronze medals in the 1984 Olympic Games, she was the first American woman ever to win an individual medal in gymnastics. In April 1985 Retton became the first gymnast to be elected to the U.S. Olympic Hall of Fame.

Tennis player Jennifer Capriati was born in New York, New York. Her father, Stefano, is an Italian immigrant. Capriati turned professional in 1990, at age 13, and in 1991 she reached the semifinals of Wimbledon and the U.S. Open. In the 1992 Olympic Games in Barcelona, Spain, Capriati won the gold medal in women's singles tennis.

The wide-ranging contributions of Italians in America are difficult to measure. Throughout this country's history, Italian Americans have established themselves as leaders in a great variety of endeavors. With imagination, determination, and spirit, they continue to enrich life and culture in the United States.

INDEX

ACKNOWLEDGMENTS The photographs in this book are reproduced through the courtesy of: pp. 2, 6-7, 11 (top and bottom), 13, 19, 20-21, 23, 64, Library of Congress; pp. 8, 14-15, 43, 44 (left), Independent Picture Service; p. 9, Charles W. Polzer; p. 10, sketch by Frances O'Brien; pp. 12, 18, 22, 26, The Bettmann Archive; p. 16, map by Laura Westlund; p. 25 (right and left), Cabrini Medical Center; p. 27, State Historical Society of Wisconsin; pp. 28-29, Tamiment Library, New York University; p. 29, 31, 36, UPI/Bettmann; p. 30, Collectors Book Store; p. 32, Ken Howard/Brooklyn Academy of Music; p. 34, Ghirardelli Chocolate; p. 35, Chrysler Corporation; p. 37, Office of the Governor of New York State; p. 37, Geraldine Ferraro; p. 38, The Supreme Court Historical Society, copyright the National Geographic Society; p. 39, Northwestern National Life Insurance Company; p. 40, Department of Special Collections, University Research Library, UCLA, Los Angeles Daily News Records; p. 41, Leo Castelli Photo Archives; p. 42, Metropolitan Opera Association, Inc.; p. 44 (right), Lawrence Radiation Laboratory, University of California; p. 45, Office of the Commissioner, copyright Roy Gumpel; p. 46, Saturday Review; p. 47, copyright 1985 Paul Glines, courtesy of New Directions; p. 48 (top), TV Times; p. 48 (bottom), NBC; pp. 49, 50 (left and right), 51, 52, 53, 55 (left and right), 63, Hollywood Book and Poster; p. 56, The Ring Book Shop; p. 57 (left), San Francisco 49ers; p. 57 (right), Green Bay Packers; p. 58, Indianapolis Motor Speedway; p. 59, copyright 1992 New York Yankees; p. 60, Photofest.

Front cover photograph, Susan L. Gregg. Back cover photograph, M. Brennecke.

This sculpted relief bust of Italian explorer John Cabot adorns the U.S. Capitol building in Washington, D.C.

Groups featured in Lerner's In America series:

AMERICAN INDIANS
DANES
FILIPINOS
FRENCH
GREEKS
ITALIANS
JAPANESE
JEWS

KOREANS
LEBANESE
MEXICANS
NORWEGIANS
PUERTO RICANS
SCOTS &
   SCOTCH-IRISH
VIETNAMESE

Lerner Publications Company
241 First Avenue North • Minneapolis, Minnesota 55401